Contents

CW00839941

Introduction

This manual is intended to be a logical successor to "Swimming - An illustrated guide to teaching the early practices". Its aim is to give guidance on teaching pupils who now have generally good technique, or who may be starting competitive swimming.

The book contains a wide range of advanced practices, which are only of value if the swimmer is competent. It is most important to select them correctly, and accurate observation and analysis of the swimmer are the key skills required by the teacher. Variety of practice is important of course, and the variety should come from controlled progression of activities, not randomly.

So: Observe ⟶ Analyse ⟶ Select

And remember ... *"Nothing is taught until it is learnt!"*

Pupils Rights

Every pupil has the right to:
- be treated with respect
- learn in safe, healthy surroundings
- have expert tuition
- be properly prepared
- participate at an appropriate level
- play as a child
- have fun in lessons
- an equal opportunity to be successful.

Safety! Safety! Safety!

Accidents often occur due to poor organisation. It is therefore the duty of every teacher to prepare thoroughly and think ahead. **Insist** on discipline.

A teacher must be in full control and be able to clear the water within seconds in an emergency.

Check pupils **ability** in shallow water first.

- Skills learnt earlier may be 'rusty'.

- They may not know what is safe in deep water.

- A distance badge does not mean 'deep water safety'.

- A costume covered with badges may be borrowed.

Practices should be just achievable. Avoid injuries by putting your pupils into ability groups.

Goggles should only be allowed when chemicals are a problem, or for medical reasons. As swimming teachers it is our job to teach pupils to use their eyes; after all they would not be wearing goggles if they fell into a river or a canal!

Jewellery should be removed.

First Aid Know where the first-aid kit is kept. Do you have a first-aid qualification? Are you up-to-date?

Telephone A telephone should be accessible. However it may be coin operated. Do you have the correct change?

Depths of the pool should be pointed out to the pupils. Head first entries of any kind must be into a depth of at least 1.8 m, or at least full reach depth of the pupils, which ever is the greater.

Equipment must be put away when not in use. Loose floats can be very dangerous and must be stored. Pupils should do this!

Horseplay in the changing rooms or on the poolside is particularly dangerous due to the wet floors. Pupils should always **walk** and keep well away from the edge of the pool.

School Travel Know your insurance. Travel with a completed register, making a head count before you leave school, and before you leave the pool premises.

Communications

Good Teaching Positions are vital. **"See and be seen by all"** - **"Hear and be heard by all"** and remember **" A picture is worth a thousand words".**

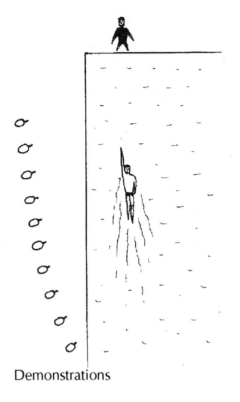

Demonstrations

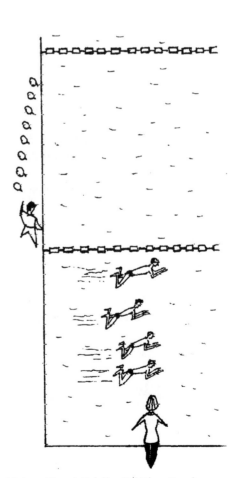

Small groups

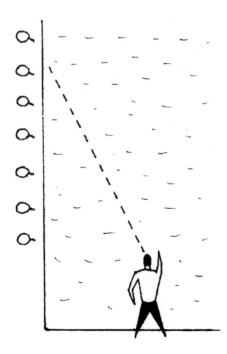

Using The Corners

Using The Middle Of The Pool

Observing and Analysing

Every teacher should be looking below as well as above the water, spotting faults, finding causes, and correcting them. To do this effectively you need a basic understanding of stroke mechanics, to the level of the ASA Teachers Course.

It is important to keep records, and record only **what you see**, not what you feel you should see.

Walk around so you can observe from the best angles.

First length:	Observe the stroke and get an overall impression.
Second length:	Look at the overall **body** position.
	Does the swimmer move smoothly?
	Is the stroke streamlined?
Third length:	Do the **legs** balance the body?
	Is the kick deep or shallow?
	Do they provide propulsion?
	From where is the movement initiated?
Fourth length:	Except for breaststroke, do the **arms** provide the main propulsion? Are there long movements with a "soft" entry?
	What path do the arms take?
Fifth length:	Observe the **breathing**.
	Is it effective? early? late?
Sixth length:	Is the **timing** rhythmical? smooth? continuous?
Seventh length:	Check the whole stroke again. Evaluate.
Remember:	**B**ody **L**egs **A**rms **B**reathing **T**iming

Practices and Faults
Dealing with faults

• Faults take time (and hence patience) to fix.

• If they are not fixed, the swimmer will compensate for them, and the stroke will not develop correctly.

• Many faults in technique are caused by other faults, for example:

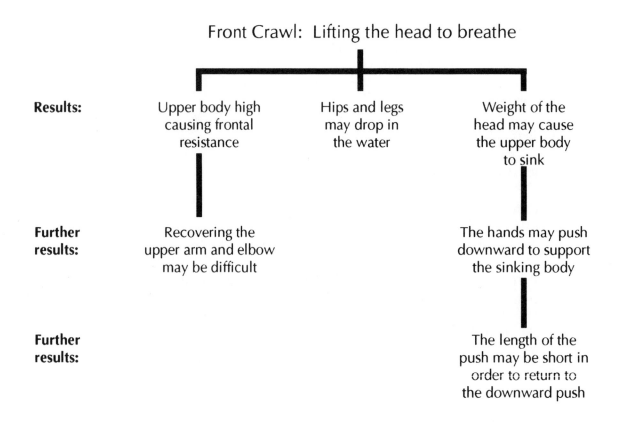

Front Crawl: Lifting the head to breathe

Results:

Upper body high causing frontal resistance

Hips and legs may drop in the water

Weight of the head may cause the upper body to sink

Further results:

Recovering the upper arm and elbow may be difficult

The hands may push downward to support the sinking body

Further results:

The length of the push may be short in order to return to the downward push

Find the cause.   Fix it!

Notes

Front Crawl

Body.

The water line should be between the hair-line and the eyes.

Rolling is a good thing:

- arms recover with less strain

- breathing is easier

- the arms get a better purchase on the water

- there is less frontal resistance as the swimmer leans into the pull. (Compare the barge-like bow wave of the breaststroker.)

Legs. The main aims are streamlining and balancing the arm action.

- Start each width or length with a strong push.

- Relaxed "long" legs swing from the hips with loose ankles. This causes in-toeing, more surface area and more drive.

- Allow the hips to roll in time with the shoulders. This helps streamlining and makes timing of the stroke more natural.

- Progress to faster deeper kicking. (You will be able to tell if the kicking is overdone because the shoulders will oscillate.)

Arms. The main aim is propulsion.

A high elbow with a "soft" hand entry (silent, thumb-first) will help to produce a good body position. Also:

- the hand will clear the water more easily

- the arm's weight will be more central, reducing sway

- the hand will be correctly positioned, ready for entry

- The hand must go INTO, not onto, the water.

Breathing

Inhaling shouldn't have to be taught - but exhaling does!

- Inhale through the mouth, exhale through the nose and mouth.

- Expel the air quickly and completely.

- Practice breathing on both sides. Have them breathe toward the same side of the pool, going down and back.

Front Crawl

Tips.

Teach at slow speed. You'll see the effect at full speed.

Develop breathing with single arm pulling:

- when the pulling arm is below the shoulder, start to exhale.

- once the breath is taken, the head returns to a central, face down position.
  (The head follows the recovering hand back to the soft entry.)

Noisy high-revvers benefit from lengths of arms only, counting their own strokes, then trying to use fewer.

Front Crawl Advanced Practices

Practice

Effects

Full Stroke

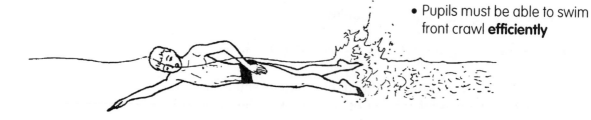

- Pupils must be able to swim front crawl **efficiently**

Legs only

Over grasp the float with head up

- Increases resistance
- Develops the kick

Kick on the side

Head resting on extended lower arm

- Helps to maintain a regular kick whilst breathing

Legs only
- Head up
- Vertical float half submerged

- Increases resistance
- Encourages harder kick

Front Crawl Advanced Practices

Practice

Effects

Single arm pulling

Back of hand strokes head on recovery

- Keeps the elbow high

- Encourages thumb first entry
- Enables the pupil to watch the pull under the water

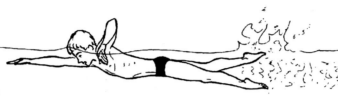

Single arm 'trailing'

Draw the thumb up the side of the body to the armpit, before stretching out to enter

- Elbow stays high

- Finger tips stay close to the surface

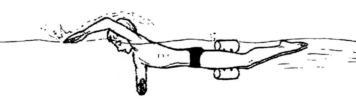

'Catch up'

- No breathing
- One arm enters and pauses until the other has pulled and caught up

- Encourages reaching for the 'catch' before pulling
- Develops a good leg kick

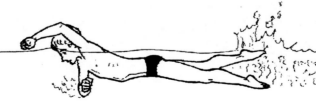

Arms only with a pull buoy

- Helps concentration on entry, pull and recovery

- Strengthens arm action

Full stroke using fists

- Pupil uses the lower arm more efficiently

- Counting strokes with and without fists enables them to compare the difference

Front Crawl Faults

CP = Corrective Practice

TP = Teaching Point

Lack of streamlining

Creates Resistance

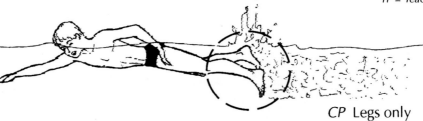

CP Legs only
TP 'Relaxed flexible ankles'

Deep kick

Creates Resistance

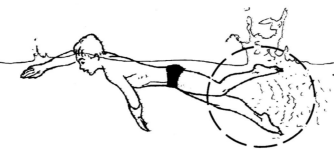

CP Legs only-thumbs linked
TP Keep a 'bubble' at the surface

Over reaching at entry

May cause the elbow to
drop and pause at 'catch'

CP Single arm pulling 'trailing'
TP 'Stroke your head and thumb
first entry'

Gliding at 'catch'

May cause late
breathing

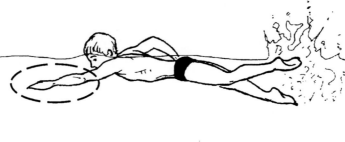

CP Bi-lateral breathing
TP 'Breathe every third pull'

Lack of roll

Poor purchase on
the water

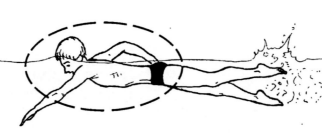

CP Single arm pulling
TP 'lean and press'

Front Crawl Faults

CP = Corrective Practice

TP = Teaching Point

Elbow leading

Loss of power from lower arm and paddle

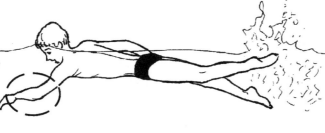

CP Fist swimming
TP 'Push the water towards your feet'

Early recovery

May restrict body roll

CP Single arm pulling
TP 'Brush your thigh with your thumb'

Straight arm pull

Causes bobbing and a weak 'lever'

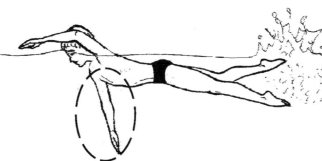

CP Fist swimming
TP 'Watch your arm pull under your nose'

Wide recovery

Causes sway

CP Single arm pulling - 'trailing'
TP 'Thumb up to your armpit'

Looking backwards to breathe

Causes poor streamlining

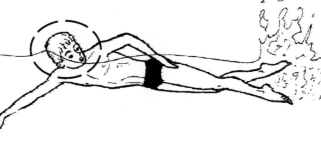

CP Bi-lateral breathing
TP 'Breathe every third pull'

Notes

Butterfly

Flexibility, grace, power and skill are required. Think of the movement of a dolphin - try to dispel ideas of pushing and pulling.

Body.
- Key skills to be taught are relaxation, feel of the water, and undulation of the whole body.

- The swimmer must think of flowing through the water.

- Imagine submerging under a floating log and emerging again.

- The head must lead the shoulders down as the hands enter the water.

Legs.
- Butterfly has the most powerful leg action of all strokes, having a continuous deep movement amplified by the body undulation. The feet together give an effective driving surface.

- The hips should stay close to the surface throughout.

- Think of the legs kicking the arms in to pull, and again kicking the head out to breathe.

Arms.
- The rounded muscles covering the shoulders are rolled inwards towards the cheeks. The shoulder blades look as if they are lifting out of the body.

- The elbows and forearms are the last to submerge, reaching for the "catch".

- Single arm pulling is a key practice. Turn the head to breathe as the arm recovers. This slight roll of the body allows the hips and thighs to stay high in the water. If this practice can be done successfully, improvement is usually rapid. If not, the swimmer will probably not progress.

- In single arm pulling, the hand finds still water away from the entry bubbles, then the arm bends as the hand sweeps out, then in, then out again, acting as a sculling blade. The pitch changes throughout.

- Recovery should start at the top of the legs. Further pushing causes tension.

Breathing.
- Have early competitive swimmers raise their chins so the windpipe is not constricted.

- Most muscles used in the pull and recovery are attached to the rib cage. Relax and keep the shoulders dropped to avoid breathlessness.

Tips.
- Find a good demonstration.

- Encourage relaxation and rhythmic strokes.

- Take care not to over-extend or tire the pupil.

- Emphasize the undulation of the whole body, starting with the head and shoulders, and moving down through the hips to the knees and ankles.

- Think of the body moving past the anchored arms.

Butterfly Advanced Practices

Practice   **Effects**

Full Stroke

- Pupils must be able to swim the stroke **efficiently**

Legs Only and Sculling

- Emphasis placed on the leg action whilst still allowing undulation

Undulation on the bottom of the pool - arms at sides

- Develops undulation
- Emphasises the upward phase of the action

Undulation on the back - arms extended

- Encourages vigorous extension of the knee

- Feet flip up to the surface
- Good hip movement

Single arm pulling

- One arm extended
- Breathing to the side

- Improves the minor kick

- Keeps hips close to the surface
- Improves entry technique

Butterfly Advanced Practices

Practice   **Effects**

Single arm pulling

Arm at side

- Pupil consciously bends his neck to direct his head and shoulders down upon entry

- Good for shoulder and neck flexibility

Porpoising

- Gives the feel of dolphin movements
- Develops confidence
- Could be used in early practices

Arms only

- Able to concentrate on entry and pull

- Head flows with the arms
- Improves the body position

Dive

- Enables the swimmer to pull and then relax

dive to repeat   pull up   3 kicks under

Pattern swimming

repeat   3 right pulls   3 left pulls   3 full stroke

- Alleviates fear of stroke
- Develops undulation

Butterfly Faults

Excess knee bend

Creates resistance and
poor undulation

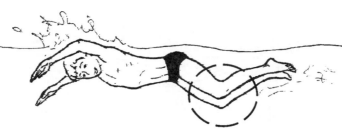

CP Legs only on back
TP 'Keep knees under water
- whip up with feet'

Late entry

Creates pause in
forward momentum

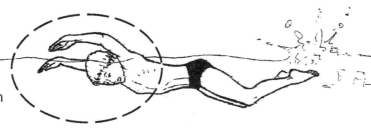

CP Single arm pulling
TP 'Fast flinging action'

Diving at entry

Excessive undulation
caused by lifting the
upper body

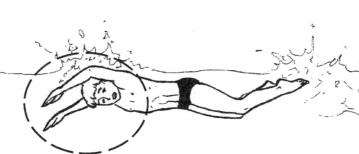

CP Full stroke no breathing
TP 'Reach forward with
'soft' entry'

High catch

Lifts the upper body
causing resistance

CP Single arm pulling
TP 'Sink to catch'

Dropped elbows

Loses power from strong
muscles and upper arm

CP Arms only
TP 'Key-hole pull'

Butterfly Faults

Wide pull

Loses power

CP Single arm pulling
TP 'Key-hole sculling
     patterns - thumbs almost
     touching'

Straight arm push

Head will lower too soon and
not synchronize with arms

CP Single arm pulling
TP 'Key-hole pulling'

High recovery

Causes excessive undulation

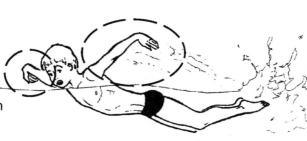

CP Full stroke no breathing
TP 'Fingertips just trail the
     water surface'

Lifting to breathe

Causes excessively undulating
legs and sculling

CP Single arm pulling
TP 'As the hand pulls level
     with the head the chin
     lifts'

Late breathing

Cause poor body position

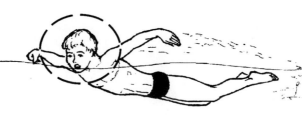

CP Single arm pulling
TP 'Head out - hands out'

Notes

Breaststroke

Body.

- Stretch the shoulders and point the toes to decrease frontal resistance.

- Keep the head still, relative to the shoulders.

Legs.

- The heels should be drawn up close to the seat. Flexibility in the hips is important.

- The kick-back sequence should be:

    - the heels press back, automatically followed by the instep and the lower leg

    - the feet rotate, producing a whipping action

    - the feet snap together, producing their own propulsion

Arms.

- Before the pull starts, the hands should be lower than the elbows.

- The hands start a sculling action, angled at 45 degrees, thumbs down.

Breathing.

- The downward press of the arms helps easy breathing.

- Lift the chin forward and upward, then breathe in through the mouth.

Tips.

- A useful practice is "Sink .. Push .. Glide .. Long pull underwater " This shows pupils how much power there is in the arms.

- Breaststroke should be a long stroke, swum without rushing.

Breaststroke Advanced Practices

Practice

Effects

Full stroke

- Pupils must be able to swim the stroke **efficiently**

Inverted breaststroke heels

- dropping down to touch fingertips

- Promotes good hip flexibility

- Allows the feet to 'catch' the water
- Develops the propulsive phase

Legs Only

- Kicking up to touch fingertips

- Decreases frontal resistance by increasing the angle at the thigh

- Promotes acceleration from the hip

Legs only

- Arms extended
- Thumbs linked

- Develops power in the leg kick

- Encourages lifting of the chin to breathe

Legs only

- Float vertical
- Half submerged

- Resistance is increased

- Strengthens the leg action

Breaststroke Advanced Practices

Practice   **Effects**

Egg beater kick

• Thumbs linked

• Builds up the inner leg strength

• If done whilst treading water pupils can watch the kick develop

Legs only

• Sculling

• The pull develops through the correct wrist movements

Arms only

• With a pull buoy

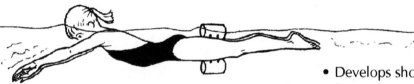

• Develops shoulder lift
• Encourages a bent arm pull

Breastroke arms – 'fly legs'

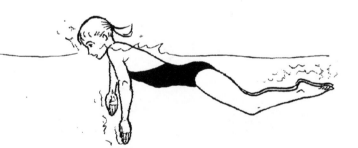

• Strengthens the arms
• Leads to undulation

Pattern swimming

2 full strokes   3 leg kicks

• Encourages good timing
• Develops a stretch of the legs prior to full stroke

Breaststroke Faults

CP = Corrective Practice

TP = Teaching Point

Heels not recovering high enough

Causes poor coordination

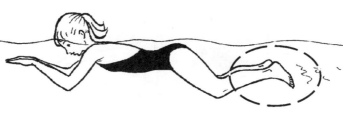

CP Inverted breaststroke

TP 'Ankles to touch fingertips'

Kicking back too soon

Ineffective propulsion and lack of drive

CP Treading water simultaneous action

TP 'Keep your neck above the water'

Wide kick back

Ineffective propulsion

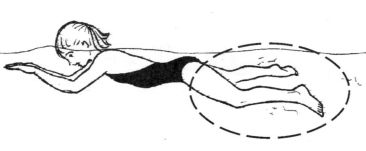

CP Legs only - heels to touch fingers

TP 'Whip back and snap ankles together'

Not snapping feet together

Results in poor streamlining

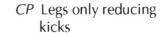

CP Legs only reducing kicks

TP 'Whip your ankles together'

Head too high

Gives profile resistance

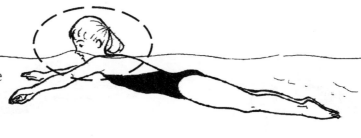

CP Full stroke

TP 'Keep your chin in the water - look at your hands as they recover'

Breaststroke Faults

CP = Corrective Practice

TP = Teaching Point

Pulling down

'Catch' will be missed and body may lift

CP Swimming with fists clenched

TP 'Feel lower arm pulling back'

Pausing at the end of the pull

i.e. a break in propulsion

CP Arms only
TP 'Press-swirl and reach'

Pulling beyond shoulders

Causes a break in continuity

CP Legs only and sculling

TP 'Can you see your hands without turning your head'

Breathing too early

Creates profile resistance

CP Legs only and sculling
TP 'Press-swirl and blow'

Breathing too late

i.e. poor timing

CP Full stroke reducing strokes
TP 'Sweep in and blow'

Notes

Back Crawl

To benefit from these practices, flexibility round the shoulders is needed. Look for the hands entering in line with the shoulders, and a good bent arm pull.

Head

- Relaxed, with the water level at the base of the ears.

- Steady, and in line with the body.

Legs

- The kick balances the sideways sweep of the arms.

- Without a strong kick the body will sway from side to side.

Arms

- A bent arm pull is needed because:

    - the arm can exert a greater force on the water

    - the force is nearer the body centre line, reducing sway

    - the hand can change pitch down the track, searching for still water.

    - There must be continuous arm action - no pauses.

Tips

- Lean into the catch:

    - the sculling action will be more effective if the hands are not too near the surface

    - lateral sway will be reduced.

- Get the little finger out first after the push:

    - this rotates the arm ready for recovery

    - it encourages roll

    - it locks the elbow of the recovering arm.

Practice   **Effects**

Full Stroke

- Pupils must be able to swim the stroke **efficiently**

Legs only on the side

Head resting on the lower arm which is extended

- Gives a feel for the water and helps synchronisation

Legs only

Hands interlocked

- Lifts the chest
- Refines the leg action
- Develops stretch

Legs only
Elbows in the water

Lower arms raised above abdomen

- Creates resistance
- Strengthens the kick

Back Crawl Advanced Practices

Practice — **Effects**

Double arm pulling and leg kick

- Develops the bent arm action and shallow push through to the hips
- Aim to reduce the number of strokes

Single arm pulling

Resting arm at thigh

- Improves technique
- Rolls to allow greater propulsion
- Encourages shoulder lift for recovery

Single arm pulling - resting arm extended above head

- Refines technique (particularly entry to catch)
- Lengthens the stroke

Catch up

Pausing beyond the head

- Develops precision of hand entry
- Improves technique
- Improves leg kick

Kicking and rolling

6 Kicks ⟶ Pull and recover to the other side ⟶ 6 Kicks

- Develops feel for roll
- For lifting shoulders to apply bent arm pull

Back Crawl Faults

Moving the head

Poor streamlining

CP Double arm pulling
TP 'Look towards your feet'

Head held too high

Creates frontal resistance

CP Legs only arms extended
TP 'Head between arms'

Over kicking

Creates resistance

CP Legs only
TP 'Toes to bubble at the surface'

Entering outside the body width

Poor propulsion

CP Single arm pulling
TP 'Brush you ear with your arm'

Back Crawl Faults

Not rolling to gain purchase on the water

Means poor application of force

CP Single arm pulling - resting arm at thigh
TP 'Roll and press'

Insufficient shoulder roll

Gives lack of power

CP Single arm pulling Resting arm extended
TP 'Lean and press'

Elbow leading instead of hand

Makes forearm and paddle ineffective

CP Double arm pulling
TP 'Press & bend'

Pulling too deeply

Symptoms: Bobbing up and down & lack of power

CP 'Catch up'
TP 'Press & bend'

Notes

Starts and Turns

Starts and turns have a significant impact on overall competitive performance. The main aims are to keep the momentum gained from the dive or push, and to start the stroke in balance.

STARTS

Safety.

Make all pupils aware of possible dangers when diving ... even obvious ones such as slipping at take-off.

The policies of the ASA (at the time of writing) on space and depth requirements are these:

Forward clearance: at least 7.6m must be available.

Diving from the side: If the pool side is not more than 380mm above the water line, the water depth must be at least 1.5m, or the pupil's full reach height, whichever is the greater.

Diving from starting blocks: Swimmers should not be permitted to dive from a starting block of a maximum height of 500mm (from the water surface) into water of the minimum depth above until they have demonstrated an ability to execute correctly the tasks outlined in the Competitive Start Award.
(This is available from the ASA Awards Centre - address inside rear cover.)

Pre-requisite skills are listed before the practices, and must be tested before further progression takes place.

"Hands On"

This position known as "Hands On"

- should be used at every entry and after every turn

- is essential for protecting the head

- helps streamlining

Racing Starts

Pre - Requisites

- All can perform a plunge dive and hold the glide for approximately 5 metres with 'hands on'

- All can push and glide on the back, front and side

- The under water to surface phase has already been taught

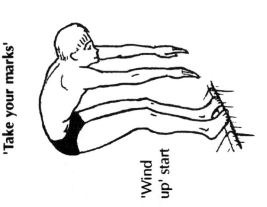

'Take your marks'

'Wind up' start

- Feet slightly apart
- Toes over the edge
- Body naturally curved
- Shoulders relaxed

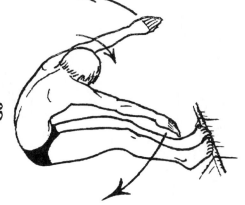

'Go'

- Shoulders and head drop **as** arms move forward and up
- Weight now transfers
- Body leans forward

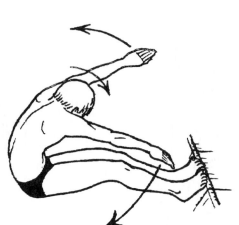

Wind up

- Knees still bending
- Head still dropping
- Body about to overbalance

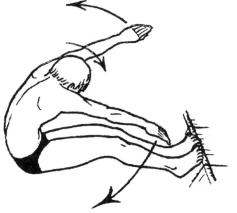

Take off

- Arms swing forward
- At same time the legs give a vigorous drive from the side

Racing Starts

Take off

- A lunge forward
- Arms move in line with body **as** legs push hard

- Arms swing sideways in a low arc
- A backward thrust from toes to fingers as dive flattens

Clean entry, 'hands on'

Head lifts slightly to avoid going too deep

Wind up

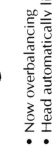

- Now overbalancing
- Head automatically lifts **as** arms swing forward

- Hips move up out of water as head moves back

Head leads as feet leave the water

'Go'

- Pull down suddenly
- Head drops to knees
- Body starts to lean

- Press down to lift up
- Hips move up

'Take your marks'

Grab Start

- Toes over the edge, apart
- Grab inside/outside the feet
- Hips always higher than head

Back Crawl Start

- Feet high, staggered
- Pull up and in
- Hips still in water

Underwater Phases: Front Crawl

- The same phase follows Starts *and* Turns
- Find a **good** demonstrator, then try and copy
- then break the skill down into small segments

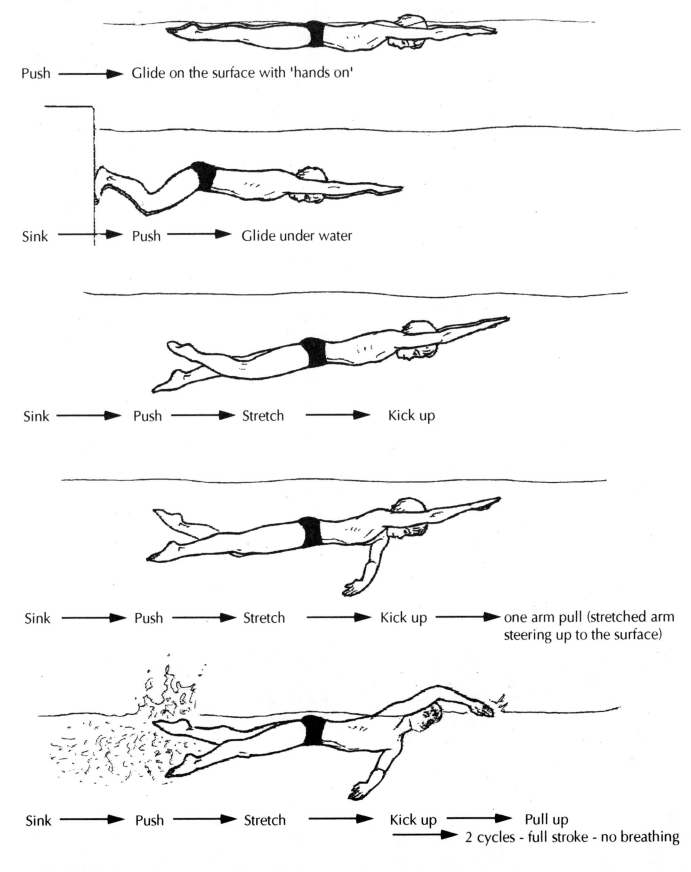

Push ———▶ Glide on the surface with 'hands on'

Sink ———▶ Push ———▶ Glide under water

Sink ———▶ Push ———▶ Stretch ———▶ Kick up

Sink ———▶ Push ———▶ Stretch ———▶ Kick up ———▶ one arm pull (stretched arm steering up to the surface)

Sink ———▶ Push ———▶ Stretch ———▶ Kick up ———▶ Pull up
———▶ 2 cycles - full stroke - no breathing

Underwater Phases: Back Crawl

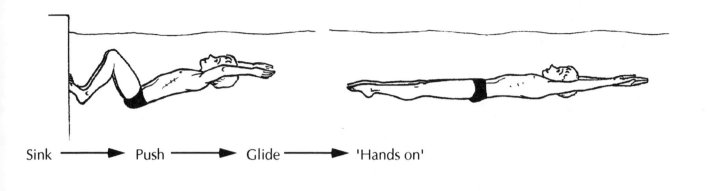

Sink ⟶ Push ⟶ Glide ⟶ 'Hands on'

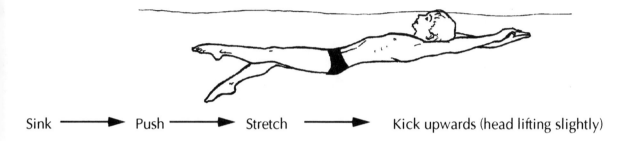

Sink ⟶ Push ⟶ Stretch ⟶ Kick upwards (head lifting slightly)

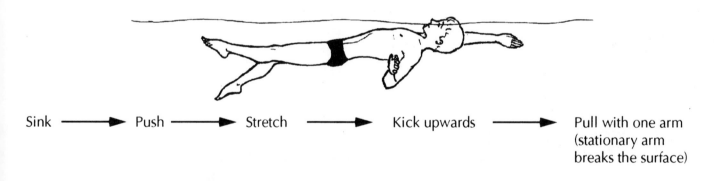

Sink ⟶ Push ⟶ Stretch ⟶ Kick upwards ⟶ Pull with one arm (stationary arm breaks the surface)

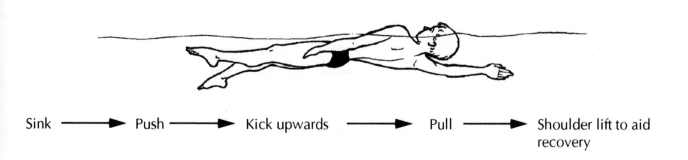

Sink ⟶ Push ⟶ Kick upwards ⟶ Pull ⟶ Shoulder lift to aid recovery

Underwater Phases:
Breaststroke & Butterfly

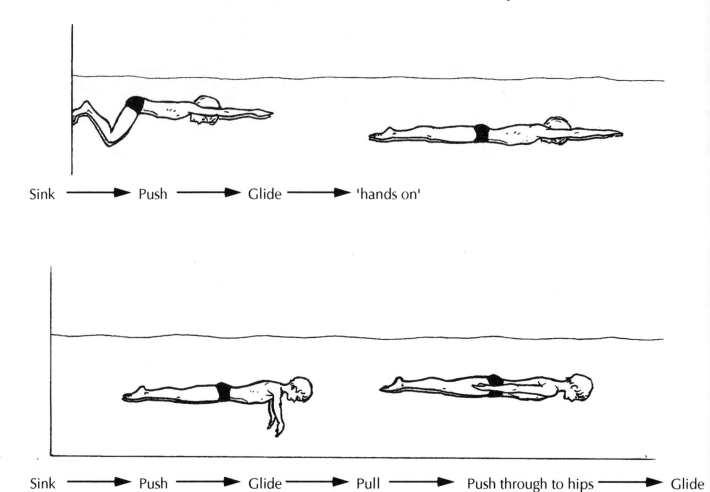

Sink ➔ Push ➔ Glide ➔ 'hands on'

Sink ➔ Push ➔ Glide ➔ Pull ➔ Push through to hips ➔ Glide

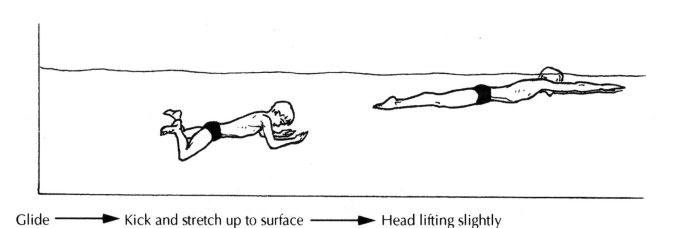

Glide ➔ Kick and stretch up to surface ➔ Head lifting slightly

For Butterfly

Sink ➔ Push ➔ Kicking upwards ➔ One pull up to the surface and into stroke

Turns

N.B. Tumble turns need a depth of at least 900mm.

Hit the wall confidently .. no hesitation! Rebound like a rubber ball.

Pre-requisites. Pupils should be able to:

- Push and glide on the front and on the back and on the side
- Do hand stands
- Do somersaults, tucked and piked...

Teaching Somersaults

Start by using arms for transfer of momentum

- Water at shoulder depth

- Crouched ready to spring forward

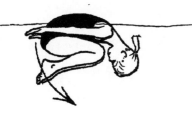

Or from a static position

- Mushroom float
- Pushing the hips up out of the water
- Rolling into a forward somersault

Result

- Tucked tight like a ball

Front Crawl Turns

Progressions **away** from the wall

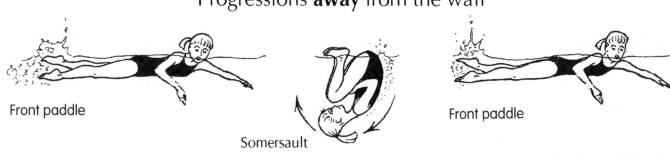

Front paddle

Somersault

Front paddle

Front paddle

1/2 Somersault

Back Paddle

Front paddle

1/2 Somersault with 1/4 twist

Kicking on the side

Front paddle

1/2 Somersault with 1/2 twist

Legs only 'hands on'

Front Crawl Turns

Progressions **into** the wall

Front paddle

1/2 somersault

Hold this position by sculling

Front paddle

1/2 somersault

1/4 twist and hold by sculling

Front paddle ➤ 1/2 somersault, then …

'Hands on'

…adding an extra twist onto front as you push and glide

Front paddle ➤ 1/2 somersault, then …

'Hands on' - full stretch - ready for underwater phase

Back Crawl Turns

Break down into small progessions once your pupils have seen a good demonstration.

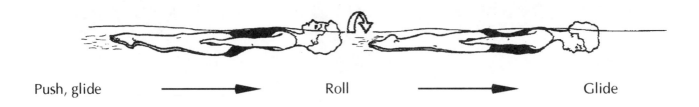

Push, glide   ⟶   Roll   ⟶   Glide

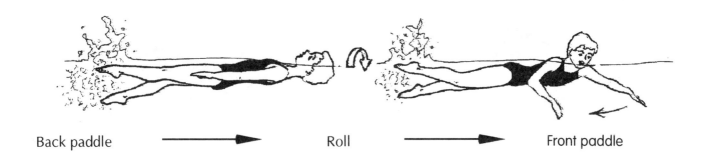

Back paddle   ⟶   Roll   ⟶   Front paddle

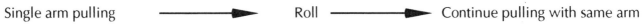

Single arm pulling   ⟶   Roll   ⟶   Continue pulling with same arm

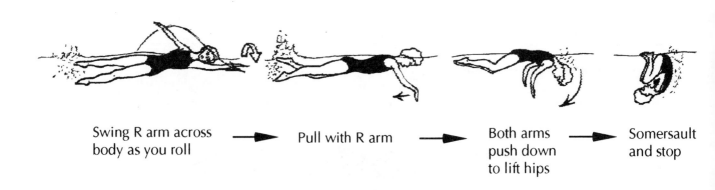

Swing R arm across body as you roll   ⟶   Pull with R arm   ⟶   Both arms push down to lift hips   ⟶   Somersault and stop

Back Crawl turns

Into the wall

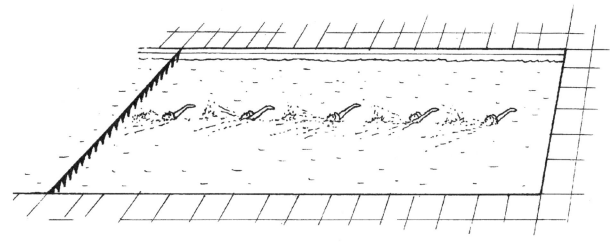

Measure how many strokes from the flags (usually five)

3 strokes from the flags ⟶ Roll

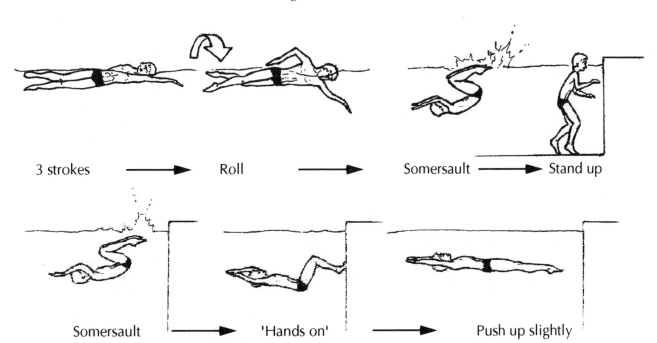

3 strokes ⟶ Roll ⟶ Somersault ⟶ Stand up

Somersault ⟶ 'Hands on' ⟶ Push up slightly

Pupils are now ready for the under water phase

Breaststroke and Butterfly Turns

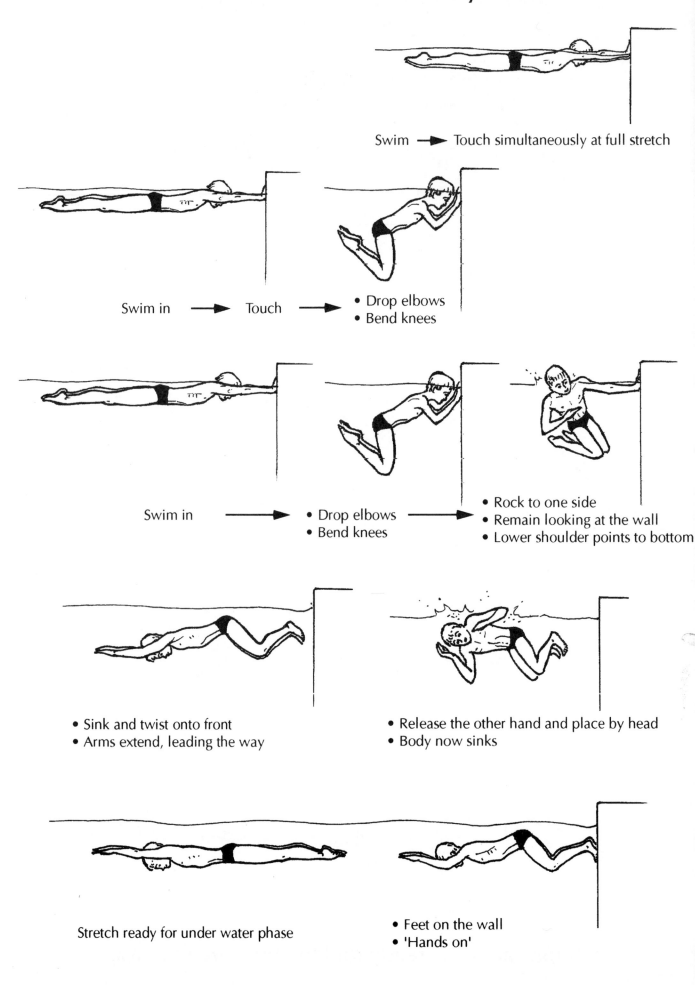

Swim ➙ Touch simultaneously at full stretch

Swim in ➙ Touch ➙
- Drop elbows
- Bend knees

Swim in ➙
- Drop elbows
- Bend knees
➙
- Rock to one side
- Remain looking at the wall
- Lower shoulder points to bottom

- Sink and twist onto front
- Arms extend, leading the way

- Release the other hand and place by head
- Body now sinks

Stretch ready for under water phase

- Feet on the wall
- 'Hands on'

Lesson Formats

Capable swimmers need challenges, and having a variety of formats prevents staleness in the lessons. The format of the lesson, as well as the content, should be dictated by the skill level of the pupils and what you are trying to achieve.

1. ORTHODOX

This is a lesson format to use when you specifically want to develop skills and strokes by the use of progressive practices and teaching points.

Points:

- Grouping should take place to cater for the wide range of abilities.

- Usually swum over short distances in order to maintain technique. In cases of extreme weakness the practice may take place over half-widths.

- Clear water space is essential for safety, and teachers should familiarize swimmers with wave formations where space is restricted. (See Managing Large Groups.)

- Swimmers should be encouraged to concentrate on technique and not on counting widths.

- Records should be kept of their progress.

2. SCHEDULE

This is the format to use when the skills are already developed, and they can follow a written schedule on a board. It is normally used so they can practice themselves, and to develop endurance.

Points:

- Swimmers should be familiar with the practices, and have no major faults.

- The average swimmer will usually swim widths to maintain technique.

- The early competitive swimmer may also swim widths but use lengths if there is space.

- The schedule should be placed so the swimmers can read it without leaving the water

- The teacher/coach assesses, encourages and corrects if necessary and may stop the group if required.

- The schedule, and an evaluation of the swimmers, should be recorded, for reference before next time.

Lesson Formats

3. TIME/DISTANCE

This format is also used to create a challenge and develop endurance. It is not a teaching lesson, but an opportunity for the pupils to achieve. It can be used as an introduction to competition.

Points:

- Targets set should just be within reach.

- Inexperienced groups work across the width.

- Early competitors should use lanes.

- The swimmers do the counting. The teacher/coach does a random check from time to time.

- The teacher/coach's main role is motivational.

- Records and evaluation should be kept for future planning.

4. RECREATIONAL

Pupils benefit from the unconscious learning that takes place in a recreational session. General watermanship is improved through the use of games, music, movement exploration and experimentation.

'Points:

- May be in groups for games, but usually individual.

- A choice of activities could be offered, and supervised!

- Safety is at a premium as the swimmers choose their own activity, so the environment is not really controlled.

- The teacher must be very alert!

NB: Permission is given to photocopy the following lesson plans freely.

Orthodox Lesson Plan

Name of Teacher . . . . Stroke . . . .

Date . . . . Lesson Time . . . . No. of Pupils . . . .

Present Ability   Weaker   . . . .

                      Stronger   . . . .

Aim of the Lesson . . . .

. . . .

Contrasting Activity . . . .

Explanation and Demonstration (when applicable)

Introductory Activity . . . .

Main Theme   Whole group have a go at full stroke

Weaker Group

Teaching Practices	**Teaching Points**
1	. . . .
2	. . . .
3	. . . .
4	. . . .
5	. . . .

Stronger Group

Teaching Practices	**Teaching Points**
1	. . . .
2	. . . .
3	. . . .
4	. . . .
5	. . . .

Whole Group 'Have a go' at full stroke, looking for the best style

Contrasting Activity ....

Teaching Practices	Teaching Points
1	....
2	....
3	....

Supervised Free Activity (if applicable)

Give an evaluation of your lesson

....

....

....

....

....

....

....

Tutor's Evaluation

....

....

....

....

....

EXAMPLES OF SCHEDULE LESSONS (Display on a poolside board)

Generally, "*a picture is worth a thousand words*" ... if it's not too difficult to draw!

Aim: Introducing Back Crawl

Widths	Practice
4	Any stroke
2	
8	
8	
2 x 4	
6	Sculling until told to stop.

Aim: Developing Back Crawl

Widths	Practice
6	Any stroke
2 x 4	Back crawl
6	Legs only (Arms above head)
6	Legs only (Arms in resistance position)
8	Full stroke ... 30 secs rest
2 x 4	Single arm pulling (Arm at thigh)
2 x 4	Double arm pulling
8	Back crawl ... Rest
	Back tumble turns until told to stop.

Time and Distance

EXAMPLES OF TIME AND DISTANCE LESSONS

The first 5 mins should be given over to explanation, the last 5 minutes to feedback of results.

TIMED SWIM

Count the number of lengths you can swim in:

20 mins (Very competent)

16 mins (Quite strong)

10 mins (Weaker)

DISTANCE SWIM

How long does it take you to swim:

800m? (Very competent)

600m? (Quite strong)

400m? (Weaker)

TIME AND DISTANCE SWIM

Can you swim the following distances in 20 mins?

400m f/c + 400m b/c (V. comp)

300m f/c + 300m b/c (Q.strong)

200m f/c + 200m b/c (Weaker)

Managing Large Groups

Remember, most accidents happen because of poor organization. Your pupils must have space.

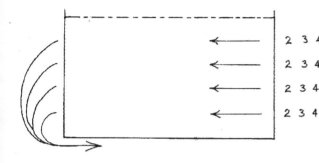

Waves.

At the start of the lesson give them each a number, and set them off in waves. However, do not demand that one wave should stay on the same practice. Each pupil should progress through the practices at his/her own speed. So a given wave could have different practices within it.

Partner work.

(It helps to have them retain the same number at each lesson.) This is useful when teaching submerging practices through partner's legs, for movement exploration, and for analysing each other's skills.

Spaced out.

For individual skills, treading water, somersaults, mushroom floats, static practices.

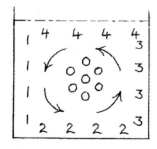

Circles for continuity.

For Personal Survival, distance swimming, and games e.g. musical hoops.

Managing Large Groups
Variations

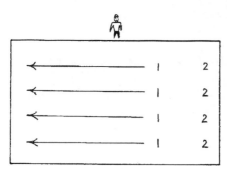

1 swims across and waits.
2 goes when 1 has touched.

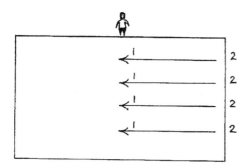

To speed things up: 2 goes as 1's feet pass halfway.

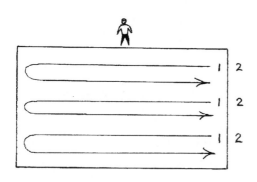

To increase the work and the rest: 2 rests while 1 swims two widths, then vice versa.

Chain Swimming: Group according to ability

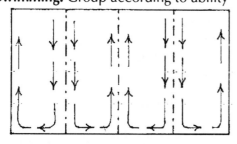

Have adjacent chains going in the same direction to avoid breaking fingers etc. Weaker swimmers can walk back.

Ensure you have a strategy for overtaking. Some options are:

- If the lane is wide enough, overtake.

- Move across to a gap going the other way, (although this disrupts the stroke).

- Have the "caught" swimmer wait at the end and allow the faster one through.

Managing Large Groups
Diving Entry

Important: Check you have at least full reach depth. Make sure they swim away from the entry point.

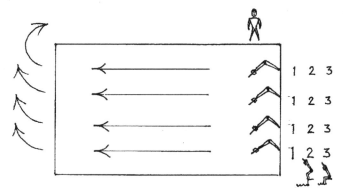

Grade your pupils. The best should go first, setting an example for those following.

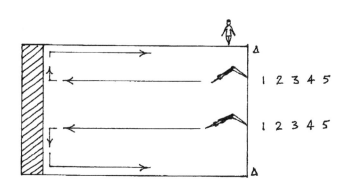

Put markers at the points where they should exit. If they are not going to swim the full width, make sure they get well away before returning.

Cannon Formation

Ideally they should be graded, the fastest going first, starting a "domino effect". Go when the **feet** of the next person have left the side. With a single row, the lead swimmer starts the formation again when the last swimmer arrives. If two rows are needed:

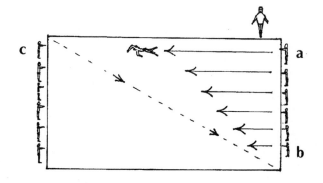

a starts the domino effect; then when **b** starts, so does **c**, starting the domino effect on that side. This can be repeated *ad infinitum*.

Notes

Preparing for Competition

Warming Up.

A warm-up session does just that: it increases the body temperature, making the muscles and tendons more elastic. This minimizes the risk of tearing during vigorous activity.

Warming down.

During exercise the muscles are helping the heart transport the blood. If this is stopped suddenly, the blood "pools" in the veins. The heart is still pumping, causing an increase in pressure, and the swimmer may feel faint or giddy. The body needs to be returned to rest in a safe manner. Also after exercise, the blood needs to be returned for "cleaning" to remove the waste products.

All this is most simply achieved by keeping the muscles moving under a light load for a few minutes.

Training and energy systems.

The body uses three main energy systems (like three different fuels) for different activities. There are systems which specialize in providing energy for short burst (starts, turns, sprinting), medium duration (swimming 100m, running 400m), and endurance activities (distance running, long swims etc.) An analogy might be the flaring of a match, the burning of a firework "sparkler", and a log or coal fire.

Training must be designed according to the event and energy system being developed. The coach must know how the swimmer will be feeling and motivate accordingly. The grid on the next page gives a summary.

Serious competitive coaching is a complex subject beyond the intent of this book. The ASA publishes the "Swimming Teaching and Coaching" series of books which gives much more information.

Energy Systems

Energy System Analogy	Effort lasts..	Swimmer feels ..	Coach must ..	Typical workout
	Seconds eg sprints	Easy!	Motivate for maximum speed	8 X 25m starting every 1m 15s
	A minute or so eg 100m swim	Pain!	Motivate for intense effort	5 X 100m starting every 5 mins
	Minutes to hours	Hard work but not painful.	Get them to find the highest speed they can maintain.	15 X 200m with 10s rest.

Floating and Sinking

What is Upthrust?

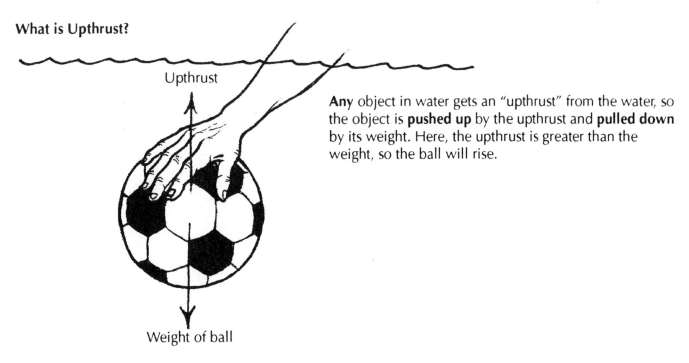

Any object in water gets an "upthrust" from the water, so the object is **pushed up** by the upthrust and **pulled down** by its weight. Here, the upthrust is greater than the weight, so the ball will rise.

Interesting Fact: (well, fairly): **The amount of upthrust is equal to the weight of the water displaced by the object.** (This was discovered by Archimedes - of Eureka fame - about 2200 years ago, and still not generally appreciated.)

Specific Gravity.

Specific Gravity (SG) is a measure of the weight of a material compared with water. For example, wood is about half (0.5 times) the weight of water; steel is about three times the weight.

If the SG is less than 1, the object floats.
If the SG is more than 1, the object sinks.

Balls same size, so upthrusts are equal

Weight less than upthrust! Ball **rises**

Weight more than upthrust! Ball **sinks**

Floating.

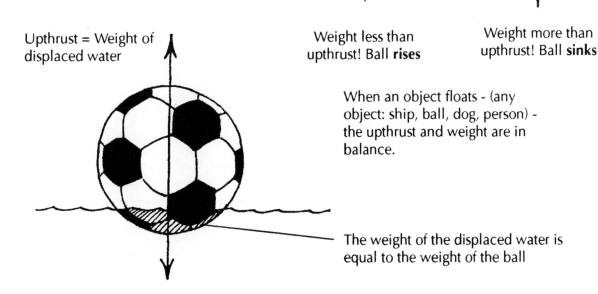

Upthrust = Weight of displaced water

When an object floats - (any object: ship, ball, dog, person) - the upthrust and weight are in balance.

The weight of the displaced water is equal to the weight of the ball

Floating and Sinking
What causes people's legs to sink?

The Centre of Buoyancy is where the **upthrust** seems to be concentrated. It is located at the "centre of volume" of the body.

The Centre of Gravity is where the **weight** of the body seems to be concentrated. It is located at the "centre of mass" of the body, usually around the naval.

With muscular, heavy legs...

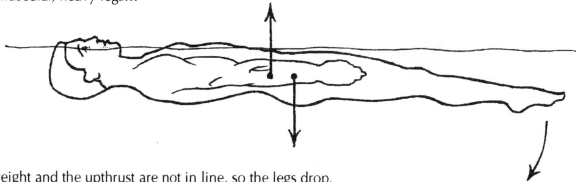

The weight and the upthrust are not in line, so the legs drop.

With more fat on the legs...

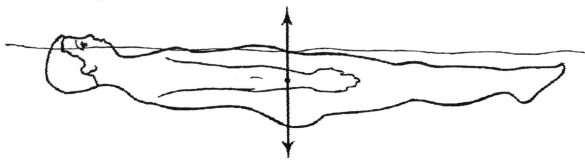

Here the Centre of Buoyancy and the Centre of Gravity are in the same place. There is no tilting action, and the body floats horizontally.

We wish you success with your teaching.   Remember ...

"If it's been well learnt, it's been well taught!"

———————— Notes ————————

Notes

Further Reading

Published by

Swimming Teaching and Coaching: Level 1	ASA
Swimming Teaching and Coaching: Level 2	ASA

Addresses (at the time of writing)

- (For awards and books) ASA Merchandising, 1 Kingfisher Enterprise Park, 50 Arthur St, Redditch, Worcestershire B98 8LG Tel: 01527 514 288   Fax 01527 514 277
- (For education and other enquiries) ASA Education Department, Harold Fern House, 18 Derby Square, Harold Fern House, Derby Square, Loughborough, Leics LE11 0AL   Tel: 01509 618 721 Fax 01509 618 701

To order more copies of this book, or its companion volumes, please send a cheque with the slip below. You get a discount if your total order is for 10 books or more. Prices include postage and packing.

Total no. of books

1 - 9	£6.50 each
10 - 29	£5.50 each
30 - 99	£5.00 each

Send to: Anne Eakin, 48 Carpenters Wood Drive, Chorleywood, Herts. WD3 5RJ.
         Tel: 01923 284 522 E-mail: rs-a_eakin@tiscali.co.uk

...✁..

    Name and address for delivery: ---

        (Please write clearly) ---

No. required

The Non-Swimmer	*getting them started*	
Swimming	*teaching early practices*	
The Competent Swimmer	*teaching more advanced practices*	
	Total books	
	Amount enclosed	£

Cheques payable to A. Eakin, please. Thank you for your order